# Meditation Archipelago

# Meditation Archipelago

POEMS BY

## Tony Leuzzi

Tiger Bark Press ❖ Rochester, New York ❖ 2018

Published by Tiger Bark Press
202 Mildorf Avenue
Rochester, NY 14609

Interior design: Richard Foerster

Cover art: Kathleen Farrell, *threehundredeightytwo*

ISBN: 978-0-9976305-8-9

Publication of this book was made possible with public funds from the New York State Council on the Arts with support of Governor Andrew M. Cuomo and the New York State Legislature.

*"The scenes of our lives resemble pictures in rough mosaic; they are ineffective from close up, and have to be viewed from a distance if they are to seem beautiful."*
>      —Arthur Schopenhauer, from *Essays and Aphorisms*
>      (translated by R. J. Hollingdale)


❖   ❖   ❖


*"O for God's sake*
*they are connected*
*underneath"*
>      —Muriel Rukeyser, from "Islands"

# Contents

## Archipelago IV: Meditation Archipelago

*Meditation Archipelago*

*Still Life*


Blue plums in the pewter bowl—
a moment seized by light and shade.

I know what you are thinking.
Someone saw this very scene, rendered

it with egg and oil, and turning
from both brush and pallet

scrubbed his hands with turpentine.
Another possibility: invented

plums, invented bowl, a gesture
of resistance at a time of deep

despair. I know what you are thinking.
Someone lost eight fingers

in a skirmish on a mound of sand.
Now he rocks in quiet rooms and with

a brush between his teeth
begins to shape, to stain a world.

# Archipelago I: And Then

*Baltimore*

When I was young, I met a younger boy named Terrence
who wrote wonderful poems
about cows. There was brown Jennifer, whose love for birds
allowed her wings to soar with
rooks to Arkansas, and Ginger, speckled silver-blue,
farting all the day in grass
while her lover perched on a rock on a hill and played
polkas on the violin . . .
Terrence was young but not so young he didn't know his
decision to write about
cows instead of Truth was a radical act, and one
I—who wrote poems of barns
because I couldn't bring myself to write about boys—
truly admired. I was still
young when I met a slightly-older girl named Carol
who draped her bed in Holstein
fleece and once drunk-dialed her mother slurring "Carol's
dead, lady, this here's Betsy."
Her boyfriend Roy was a smoking red-hot closet 'mo
and I obsessed over him
for two cold years, until he and Carol cried uncle
and he moved to Baltimore
where, I'm told, he married, divorced, came out, remarried
and now he and his husband
are looking to adopt a third greyhound, which I hate
knowing because I had big
plans for Roy involving jockstraps and a rawhide rope.
I don't know about Carol
but Terrence became less young when he began writing
poems about important
themes like Poverty and War and I was sad because
these efforts had less power
than the free unfettered bovine odes of yesteryear.
My barn poems were nothing
to speak of and I'm pretty sure no one will miss them

though I remember Terrence
gifting me a cow noisemaker when I completed
a sequence of crowned sonnets
that began "On Sunday I strolled by a rotting byre."
At the time I believed it
a masterpiece worthy of Donne or Richard Wilbur,
neither of whom Terrence knew
when I asked if he sensed their influence on my work,
but as unbelievable
as his not knowing seemed, I didn't doubt the naïf-like
power of his ignorance
nor the untutored grace that spurred him to say "Let's try
something utterly pointless."
That's when we removed our socks. He handed me a green
crayon, chose red for himself
and on the backs of poems we traced our naked feet.

## My First Memory

A
hospital room:
I am in father's arms
reaching

for
the white marble
of my twin brother's neck
just as

he—
held by mother—
reaches for mine. How long
do we

stay
wingless cherubs
suspended by an un-
seen thread?

## *Centerpiece*

Not
my best moment—
hopping a neighbor's fence
at night

when
everyone I
waved to in daylight was
sleeping

or
peeling back sheets
for a night of fitful
turning.

There
in that bed of
too many roses I
snipped free

the
fullest of them
to arrange in a vase
that stood

in
the center of
a table otherwise
empty.

## Short Story

Once, at a used bookstore in Erie, I met a blonde
needlepointist from Duluth
who had driven east in a maroon station wagon
to see her only brother
at the Gate of Heaven Cemetery. I had been
to Blain, where my third sister
shut herself in the closet of a blue bungalow
with the family photos
so I felt comfortable asking the needlepointist
if people who do needle-
point are called needlepointists. She didn't have a clue
what I was talking about
because I asked her in French, but she adored my teeth
and I her bones and since words
get in the way of such things, we didn't bother with
anything else, except to
clarify which of us should enter the restroom first
and once inside, how to make
the most of its crammed space. One hates watching people leave
used bookstores empty handed.
That is why, after we buttoned and zipped, I grabbed Kant's
*Prolegomena* and she
a retrospective edition of Cape Dorset prints.
Leaving together, I tailed
her wagon to the cemetery, where her brother
sells pink and white carnations.
"It's the only job I could find," he complained, but I
was overjoyed to see him
alive. It is more than I can say for my sister
whose episodes at the blue
bungalow ceased six years ago and all that remains
is the album, one photo
after another of children garbed in bitter greens
and laughing golds, like a stitched
cluster of asters in the draperies of autumn.

## Word Problem

The
distance between
Town A and Town B is
ninety-

five
kilometers.
At 2:14, a car
from Town

A
and a truck from
Town B barrel towards each
other.

If
the car is red
and the truck is yellow
which one

more
resembles the
brilliant glare of flowers
left with

coins
and photographs
beside the crosses of
the dead?

## *After Watching Marco Berger's* Hawaii

I won't say a word
        about pineapples.
                I will only tell you

when clear water
        pours from an outdoor spigot
                you want it to wash over you

the way it washes over
        the pale, chiseled torso
                of a man whose eyes are

the eyes of a child, that when
        he and another man stand
                beneath a giant banyan—

backs lapping the stippled
        light through its branches—
                you forget what you learned

about movement and progress
        and let each word of the sentence
                you were about to utter dissolve

one letter at a time
        while still on the tongue,
                like an unleavened wafer.

And why not? How long
        has it been since you tasted
                wonder and called it silence?

# And Then

A woman wrapped in terrycloth
leans beyond her window, shouts

*Geppetto* through an arm of birch.
He passes underneath my hand, arches

spine to concave palm
and for a brief unhurried moment

all is velvet fur, damp earth,
September's smoky air and then

that day in blue obedience:
I told my friend to close his eyes,

left him counting *seven, eight . . .*
while I—a silent, creeping thing

hidden by a screen of loosestrife—
watched him as he opened them.

No
givens, only
the imagination,
a dreamed-

up
dream, a story
borrowed from another
story

read
on a plane to—
no, that is another
story.

Fine:
I'll change the names
to protect everyone.
No one

will
hurt anymore.
No crying and pointing
it was

you
who did this, you
who made me what I am,
what I

fear
from everyone
and can't bear to see in
myself—

no.
No more givens
or assumptions. Only
a gold

ring
of dust around
the ashtray, three pencils
with worn

down
erasers and
a tin lampshade tilted
like a

green
fedora on
the head of an uncle
from Queens.

## *Bodega*

This is a poem about Stanley
who is twelve and hates his father.
Most twelve-year-olds
learn to loathe the men who
made them: Stanley started
minutes after he was born
when two cold and blistered hands
snatched him from the placid bed
between his mother's breasts.
Sooner or later each of us yearns
to grope an edge of memory
but since the girls that Stanley knows
do not yet have those pillowed swells
he steals into a bodega
on Sixth to watch Miah
the blonde thirtysomething cashier
sell soda and lotto tickets
to every weary stripe of life
'til Sandro climbs the basement stairs
and screams get lost you little shit.
Stanley flees, remembering
those rounded mounds
that bounced as she stood
on tip-toe to reach
a carton of unfiltered Camels
and swayed like bagged melons
when she stooped to grab a fallen nickel.
Later, in bed, Mia tells
the guy she's seeing about her
mother's first mastectomy. But the moment
his head hits the pillow
beside her she is facing a dark wall
dreaming of Stanley. If only
she could take him in, raise him
to be the kind of man who

loves women and will let a woman
love him back, a man
who turns to her and says
tomorrow let's ditch work and learn
the angles of our searching faces,
memorize each line and curve
so when one leaves the heat
of this bed, the other can
trace their image in air.

## Green Dolphin Street

My heart's aflutter, a noun of noun, whisper of cloud, anthology of inflorescence in which the muscle is not for a moment permitted to cease its systolic-diastolic rhythms. I am so thankful I could kiss the ground, itself an index of distractions. On Green Dolphin Street blue pigeons explore the innards of a shattered Steinway B, clearly unaware of Horowitz who would have wept to see such wreckage. On the other hand, he might have thrilled to see them roosting in the remnants of its soundboard, as if like love they planned to stay.

## *Fortune Cookie*


"You will jump a thousand puddles."
I take this metaphorically, steering clear of street
encounters, watching what I say in bed.
Sometimes something must be said, because silence
itself is a puddle one jumps when it isn't mined like silver.
Say something: A boat

grows in Brooklyn. A forest is a pad of paper. O, Boat
of easy origami, sailing on a filthy puddle,
I name you Lady Hi-Ho-Silver
in honor of an aging stripper. The street's
no place to leave a lover. Silence
kills. Soundbite: What you do in bed

connects everyone everywhere. In bed
we act out folded dreams, sail like boats
the greedy silence
of sleep, the ocean a puddle,
a pathway, a street.
Should I say a thing or two about silver

or keep that story like a sack of silver
tucked away?  I hopped in bed
with a boy from the country to forget the streets.
He came from wheat, knew nothing of boats.
When I said let's puddle
jump our way to Heaven, his silence

was the silence
of one who believes all is possible with silver
and a lick of luck. He wasn't a puddle
but I jumped him anyway. Out of bed
I drew a dozen boats—
sleek prams penciled red, sailing narrow straits,

wide oceans, thousands of miles from the street
where we met. On the silence
of paper once a forest boats
are dreams I mine like silver.
My bumpkin moved to Washington. In bed
I wonder: east or west? Memory is one more puddle.

A boat is balanced on a puddle.
The street strips all except our silence.
Instead of silver, add "In bed" to every fortune.

*Sablefish*


It should be noted that in speaking of the white flesh
of the Pacific Sable-
fish there is likely no intended contradiction
for the white of the black fish
is ironically as un-ironic as a scene
in which two broke college guys—
avowedly straight—remove their shirts and at some out-
of-shot director's bidding
begin kissing, licking, their hungry hands wandering
over tanned hairless torsos
sculpted with muscle, until one set of hands drops down
and unzips one pair of shorts
and the action is repeated by the other set
of hands on the other pair
of shorts and their cocks emerge as blushing obelisks
each swallowed by an eager
mouth that only minutes before boasted of fucking
women, the sucking leading
to fucking, a turn-taking activity where both
demonstrate remarkable
versatility for the promise of cash, which they
receive once the cameras
and girl-on-girl porn are turned off, once the tangled clothes
are gathered and they resuit
then depart warily for Microeconomics . . .
for that which is is itself
and is also the other, which one claims it is not.

*Swath*

I
thought his gift strange—
a long wool scarf in the
middle

of
May. I thought it
stranger still that one week
later—

once
the soft purple
of early vanguards had
given

way
to a brazen
swath of crimson tulips—
a hoar

frost
covered the stems
and stamens and all bright
turned black.

# The Plaque

says "Nothing Happened on This Spot
in 1832." In 1832, this spot

was maple, ash, and jagged stone—
some morels, maybe chanterelles, a spot

of dill and purple cosmos introduced by passing feet.
Whoever crossed here might have spotted

thirsty herds of fallow deer or gathered
dovetail arrowheads. It was on a spot

like this I followed father through
his fields, searching for the perfect spot

where we would dig to China. With spade
I worked beside him when three spots

of red became the sky. I woke up burning
in my bed, his hand cold upon my brow, a spot

of moonlight slanting in. *Father, did we get to China?*
*No*, he whispered, *nothing happened.* On that spot

he built a well. I knew then I must dig without him—
a little deeper every time, and always in a different spot.

## September Song

It is not necessary to gather every leaf of sorrow. It is not necessary to invent new sufferings for the precious few that have escaped our notice. At Red's Grocery, hands pick through crates of meager apples, while a palmist in the room upstairs lets fingers slip from her fingers. If the actual is to be catalogued, we must improvise reality, as if it were a garland made of green construction paper.

## Surfacing

Six
decades after
playing James Dean's heartthrob
side-kick

in
*Rebel Without
a Cause,* Sal Mineo
is still

the
first Sal who pops
up on my late morning
Google

search.
I am looking
for a boy from tenth grade
swim class

who
cried as he came
in my hand. Not a soul
can know

he
said. I agreed
because he wanted me
once and

once
was more than I
deserved. Twenty-five years
later

his
name surfaces
only after a few
dozen

black-
and white photos
of Sal lifting weights in
a west

coast
gym and one torn
but breathtaking headshot
on which

is
written "To Don—
I shall never forget
Houston."

## *Lines*

You know that old game
where you take a sheet
of legal paper,
list the names of all
the people you've had
sex with and if you
need to turn the page
to continue you're
officially a
slut? Well, today I
tried to remember
every encounter
I've ever had which
for the most part I
was able to do
though not without some
struggle with certain
names presuming I
ever knew them and
not without a tinge
of regret for those
I never called or
whose digits I did
not bother to keep
especially those
with whom the sex might
have been improved with
practice as well as
those who appear in
my dreams albeit
slightly modified
or conflated with
others I *would have*
had sex with given
the chance and who might

as well be counted
too—but as I turned
the page I wondered
how many times my
name, if I gave it,
might have appeared on
a list like this and
if I were someone's
*would have* guy and if
in terms of the game
I had won or lost.

## Haiku from the Other Hand

—for Joe Brainard


I tried to warn you,
bird, the window was closed, but
the window was closed.

❖   ❖   ❖

Unfinished crossword
on the table next to mine.
3 down: "companion."

❖   ❖   ❖

"Hello." "Hi, my name—"
"For English, press 1, Spanish
press 2." I press 6.

❖   ❖   ❖

I love wallpaper
when it isn't plastered on
the insides of vans.

✦  ✦  ✦

There can only be
one flower in this valley
and it is scarlet.

✦  ✦  ✦

March acts like a boy
who won't take his prescription
mood stabilizers.

✦  ✦  ✦

Mechanical bull—
seat of raunch and beery shouts—
you're "Out of Order."

◈   ◈   ◈

There is no reason
for anyone to play harp
in my living room.

◈   ◈   ◈

His voice is a drug.
I don't do drugs anymore—
but I remember.

◈   ◈   ◈

Let's say Stendhal wrote
six novels about the life
and times of Stendhal.

❖   ❖   ❖

Could you imagine
introducing yourself as
someone *in stemware?*

❖   ❖   ❖

When the station master
shouts "All aboard!" six people
disembark the train.

## *What I Wanted from* The Brothers Karamazov

Each character to have one and only one name

The full text of Ivan Fyodorovich's inscrutable article

Two or three Troika scenes

An aria sung by Stinking Lizaveta

A fourth son, preferably a non-neurotic savant who makes coffins and whistles

The suppressed dreamlife of Father Zosima

Victor Hugo to appear as a character

Fyodor Pavlovich to return as a ghost and continue his stream of shameless antics

A torrid tryst between Alexey and a handsome soldier

Smerdyakov to receive a full scholarship to the University of Moscow

A change of scenery, perhaps a boating trip along the Volga or a walking tour of Novgorod

Grushenka changed to a bowl of red onions

The author revealed as a trumpeter swan

A philosophical treatise on lilacs

A complimentary samovar

A sequel

## By a Bend in the River

When at a station on the Dnieper only shall the suitcase have reality, as evinced entirely in mute farewells. When in the waters of eloquence only shall the Seine seem still, as expressed in brief pantomimes of air. When on a raft along the Mississippi only the knapsack shall be saved, as suggested through serendipitous driftwood. When at a meander on the Sungari only arc shall be oxbow, as performed on a June night by reliable circles of history . . .

*Memo*


Dear
Microsoft Word—
we at the Permanent
Office

are
concerned about
antisemitism.
Any

time
we type it your
program autocorrects
it with

a
hyphen that breaks
anitsemitism
into

two
words: anti- and
Semitism. We were
told your

spell-
check understands
real words as they appear
in well-

known
dictionaries
but Semitism is
not a

word
when severed from
its negative prefix
and thus

in
no way hyphen-
appropriate. It can
not stand

on
its own either
in the wilderness or
in the

land
we were promised
by God before Micro-
soft Word

spell-
checked its way in-
to the hearts and minds of
millions.

How
many millions—
five?, maybe six?—coming
to terms

with
historical
fact have witnessed the word
they've typed

change
before their eyes
to that which is not real
and there-

fore
incapable
of having ever been
the truth?

# Raisin Bran and Sliced Tomatoes

"I must be mad," I tell myself. This morning
just before I woke, Michel Foucault
called me to the kitchen of my youth and asked
"Which sandwich do you want for lunch?" One
was ham with pepperjack, the other sliced tomatoes.
Michel was played by Morgan Fairchild.

The last time I saw Morgan Fairchild
she was scheming her way through an evening
soap called "Fashion House," slinging tomatoes
and marble cheesecake at Bo Derek. Foucault—
who once wrote, "There is not one
but many silences"—would not have asked

to change the channel. He might have asked
which one was which. "Morgan Fairchild,"
I'd explain, "is the ageless one
with style and cheekbones." "Ah, good evening
Morgan," Foucault
would say to the screen, "you look lovely in tomatoes."

"No, Bo Derek is wearing tomatoes
over a pound of peach concealer." What, he would ask,
was she concealing? "Foucault,"
I'd sigh, "you, unlike Morgan Fairchild,
are best savored in bits, a line or two with morning
coffee, like an impossible crossword, one

arresting difficulty at a time." "More than one
person," he would say to his tomato
sandwich served with morning
coffee, "writes to have no face." "Asked
and answered," I might add: "Look at Morgan—
isn't she beautiful?" But Michel Foucault

would google Michel Foucault
and reading of his death cry out, "Must one's
truth be a visible secret? I was once a child,
too, an unripe fruit who sliced tomatoes
over raisin bran and never asked
why answers only arrive in the morning."

It's almost morning now, Michel Foucault.
You have asked one question too many.
Have a tomato. And say goodnight to Morgan Fairchild.

# Archipelago II: Novaya Zemlya

## *Novaya Zemlya*

Lately, I've been thinking again about Novaya Zemlya—
that boomerang-shaped archipelago jutting from mainland Russia
like a plume from the hat of one of Chekhov's Vankas
or a molted quill writing steel vessels trapped in ice
while radioactive reindeer scatter scarred mountains and planes.
I used to see it as a crooked finger rising out of the Arctic
beckoning me with the promise of two
bright bungalows in a prairie of red grass, one department store
in Belushya Guba selling robin's egg blue bowlers
when dignified doctors insisted on black because
black is forever, like the Widow Unn and her thirty-two owls—
one stacked on top of the other as a breathing totem pole.
I imagined people from the north island Severny having nothing
to do with people from the south island Yuzhny
and if it weren't for the Matochkin Strait between them
they'd have slaughtered each other years ago. My first story
was Thomas of Severny pining for Rita from Yuzhny.
A polar bear named Isaac carried their forbidden letters
back and forth on his four-sailed schooner. Isaac didn't mind
playing pander, though there was nothing
Thomas or Rita could do except fast each morning.
Over time, both found themselves falling for Isaac, upholding
the grand fiction of their starving ardor
so he could continue from one to the other.
At seven, I received a Rand McNally map of the world
and was instantly drawn to places near the margins:
Svalbard dangling over Norway like a sprig of mistletoe—
New Zealand falling from Australia like an astronaut his shuttle—
and, of course, Novaya Zemlya, that Cézanne brush stroke, dash
of jaunty elegance, a scythe cutting water, an open
parenthesis, as if the Kara Sea began a dream that would not end.
Someday I'd live there in absolute splendor, separated
but close enough for weekend trips to Finland. I would build
my own house—a green, three-story colonial
with white trim and a balcony facing Murmansk. I would

bed all winter with Jack the Husky, two puffins
named Walter and Anne, and that unnamed goat
from a page in *Crusoe*, before Crusoe could strangle it.
By suspending "now," dismissing its facts,
there was a place I could live and belong in the world.
On March 3, 1984, I delivered a five-minute oral report
on the indigenous Nenets, those brown hunters
of foxes and seals who come and go
with the turning of weather. We had to pick an island cluster.
Jason chose Hawaii; Michael, Indonesia; Jennifer,
Galapagos, No one cared what anyone found.
On July 17, 1596, Dutch explorer Willem Barents said
you could talk to God in Novaya Zemlya, for He
would hide in such a place, withholding His secrets
from cities and men. Barents overwintered there
spooning heated cannonballs until he died
the following June. Michael covered civil war. Jennifer
rambled on about turtles. Years later, when I read
Kurt Vonnegut, I thought of her standing before us
in a plaid jumper sweating like a Slavic wrestler. O, the tears
we might have wept! But Jason sneezed
and made us laugh. "I did it for her," he whispered
in my arms as I dreamed. "She couldn't bear
another second." On October 30, 1961, Khrushchev
ordered the detonation of Tsar Bomba, the largest
nuclear weapon in human history. 500 miles away
24 Soviet soldiers watched from a shore of the Arkhangelsk
Oblast, their stiff cocks standing at attention as a ball of fire
turned to cloud and tore at pleasure with rough strife.
IMDb says *Novaya Zemlya* is a bleak thriller.
Prisoners are spared state sanctioned death for the sake
of a social experiment. All goes horribly wrong
the way social experiments do at 74° N, which is why
instead of watching it, I began my own experiment
called *Novaya Zemlya*, but was neither suited nor inclined
to meet the architectonic challenges of novel writing.
I remember my terrific first sentence: "Here
there would be no marriage or football."

But when I considered 2,500 people eking existence
in government bunkers, I felt something—
not quite guilt, closer to compassion—
and saw myself presiding over why-not weddings
and structuring game days for rudderless children.
Maybe, if I'd turned the novel upside down I could have
finished it, but I'm more of a poet. When I stand
this poem on its head, I remember my father
planting eight silver maples at the edge of our land.
He knows he is dying (eleven months the doctor says)
but keeps this morsel to himself. March rain. I shiver
beside him, wishing I hadn't insisted on holding
his shovel each time he bends to mix peat with soil.
Three years after his exit, what he planted will be twice
as tall, branches extending so wide the trees will begin
to touch one another. They will never be silver.
When I tip this poem on its side, I am stepping
my name in snow, asking myself if someone
somewhere else is, too, wondering what I will do
now that I know I am and always will be lonely. I don't
imagine I will cry, since loneliness is a nesting doll, a white
angel in a red devil and inside the angel
a tiny apple painted gold. Lately, I've been
thinking about rectangular suns, the high refraction
of light between atmospheric thermoclines,
of horizon warped as hourglass—in other words, Art.
The world needs more rectangular light, more
orange rivers, purple leaves, more
folded homes and pocket cliffs. More silver.
When I stand this poem on its feet it asks a riddle: How
do you find your way out of the forests of Novaya Zemlya?

*Archipelago III: This Is Not an Exit*

❖   ❖   ❖

Zero plus zero equals zero.
No zero is identical to
another: any zero added
to zero is a discreet zero—

an individual example
within a single category,
like a twin who shares his DNA
with another who is another;

and the third zero emerging from
the equation is brother and son
of the zeros that formed it. In this—

as in most narratives, be they
mathematical or otherwise—
there looms the shadow of Oedipus.

About two years ago, on the grounds
of The Mattress Factory, I saw
a cluster of beheaded statues,

spectral, expectant, as if waiting
for me to give them advice or scrub
the layer of green from their granite.

I snapped a picture because that is
what I do when I'm confronted with
strangeness too tangled and beautiful
to be forgotten. Then I forgot

about the picture, observed twenty-
six months of anger and ignorance,
and found it stored on my phone today
in an album called "For Later Use."

The headline says, "Take our little quiz
to discover how little you know
about what's going on in the world."

I don't need a quiz to tell me this
but I try it anyway. To my
surprise, the only answer of which
I am certain is the one I get

wrong: it was volleyball not missile
testing our satellites spotted on
a base in North Korea. It's good,
they say, to learn the facts. Volleyball

hasn't been weaponized yet but
next door, in a neighbor's apartment,
a father rages at his daughter.

Don Rickles dies. Trump bombs Syria.
A student who likes to talk instead
of write hands me *Voices of Nature*—
the collected verse of L.V. Hall.

L.V. was a blind romantic who
wrote "I love you, / for all your flowers /
and your thunders too." Much of *Voices*
is dated and awkward but I would

trade the bulk of our world's poetry
for those three lines, would trade the spring snow
to hear a side-splitting joke about
something too soon to be funny. Bomb:

see, that's a funny word. My student
says "Turn to the poem called 'Fragment.'"

Paola Clemente's heart gave out
among the rows of twisted grape vines.

Each morning, long before sunrise, she
climbed out of bed and onto a bus
that drove her to an endless harvest.

Her face was round, her fingers thin
and nimble. Never was a grape too
small it evaded her extraction.

At a table in London, someone
sips the fruit those fingers found, then laughs
when called upon to laugh. It is work

being witty, reacting to wit,
work pretending the vintage isn't
more buoyant when you taste the effort.

Blesiloquent—to speak with a lisp
or stammer. From the Latin *blæsus*
which also means stammer and therefore
a circle instead of a road. On

mornings when my cheeks are puffy
I stand before a mirror mouthing
gossoon, bullimong, heimganger, kench,
scamandering into some selcouth

state of innocence before laughter
or courage assert themselves like shields
against the saturate of certain
sounds. It's something more than exercise.

No one wants to be a bag of damp
waffles dragged through the valley of time.

I don't want to die of anything.
In forty-six more years, I still want
health, wealth, and plenty of solitude,

the occasional romance, fresh fish
each evening, rooms that smell of basil
in summer and cedar in autumn.

And I want to learn Polish and read
Polish poems, translate them into
my language and read them. Look closer:
Can you see a flaw in the blueprint?

There's a canyon between intention
and error. When you call out your name
it comes home with a hole in its shoe—
and two stories too awful to tell.

Steve Stephens shot himself today
two days after he murdered a man
named Robert Godwin, a murder he
recorded and posted on Facebook.

I'm not convinced this is the best way
to begin a poem, much less a
sonnet—albeit an unrhymed one—

in which some assertion, however
unwelcome, is developed and turned
on its awful head to affirm that
love abides beyond change, beyond death.

When I can't affirm, I attempt to
confirm: Cleveland, Eerie, McDonald's
fries. No one knows why Steve shot Robert.

Begin with an object. Okay, take
this saltshaker: its transparent shell
is scratched and scarred beyond redemption

but the salt inside it's white, whiter
than a laundered towel. Salt feels sad
when surrounded by squalor. It wants
a hand to tip its cage, so it can—

like some long-recessed memory that
suddenly emerges when it has
received a source of stimulation—

pour free, like Sam and me in a dark
theatre, his roving hand, my thigh
against his, some caper on the screen,
and, later, laughter, then a towel.

When I was twenty-one, a psychic
took my palms and closed his eyes: your soul,
he said, is ancient: you were a monk
who lived in a cave with a falcon.

He was handsome. I believe he knew
I wanted him and that his knowing
changed the reading: one day a woman
offered herself, you turned her away.

I withdrew my hands. He snatched them back.
You can't, I said. He replied, You have.
No one knows where she went when she left
but the world became a maze of loss.

I paid. We undressed. Later, alone,
a giant bird winged from my shoulder.

"This Is Not an Exit" has been hung
on a door that, in its former life,
before the sign was mounted to it,
might have been designed as an exit.

I think about this seconds before
Terry Tempest Williams steps on stage
and reminds us, "Independence is
happiness"—Susan B. Anthony.

Her grandmother gave her a dollar
to memorize that sentence. She did
of course, and never spent the dollar.

After the presentation, dozens
stand in line for her signature. I
approach the door and try its handle.

He sawed the bottoms off extinguished
extinguishers, mounted metal crowns
to their heads, and hung those crowns with chords.

Each bell—for that is what he called them—
came with a mallet, carved from fallen
branches of birch. "I didn't plant it,"
he said. "Two Latvians owned the house

before me. The woman died, the man
painted her on enormous panels
and burned them. Then he'd spray the blazes

down with sodium bicarbonate
and dump the casings in the basement.
Who knows where he went, but there they were
stacked like bricks. I had to do something."

Brick by brick, for more than fifty years,
one man builds a Cathedral of Faith.
Some say he's mad, others eccentric.
The work is endless, the progress slow.

But there is progress. Go online, see
for yourself. For myself, I ponder
a friend who writes two or three poems
a day. Some are terrific, others

awful. None are dull. His vocation—
I believe that is the proper word—
is propelled by a force too fervent

to contain or circumscribe. "My goal
in writing is to write. Or else," he
sighs, "I would have to pray to something."

Stravinsky's *Piano-Rag* sounds like
Joplin pounding "The Entertainer"
while trying to pass a kidney stone.

There is pleasure in this confluence
which at first seems absurd, like coating
sautéed liver and onions with brown

sugar and insisting it's ice cream,
an indulgence called refinement that,
with time, reveals its reasons and truth—

like the brazen atheist artist
who places ball caps on the heads of
backyard Madonnas, not, as critics

claim, to celebrate his disregard
but to shield them from the brutal sun.

Weeks ago, an end-of-winter wind
uprooted my neighbor's magnolia
which, after decades of flowering,
was tipped over and taken for dead.

She wept. I said I'd saw it down. But
because the roots were raised with earth
intact around them, the tree began
a second, sideways life: new buds formed

on its branches. When I suggested
that pulleys could be used to stand it
she clasped her hands and closed her eyes—

a gesture more performed than felt,
for I suspect she had already grieved
and pictured in its place a willow.

This morning I ate two poached eggs, one
banana and three buttered toast points.
There was no juice so I drank a glass
of tap water and studied a map

of the world's largest garbage islands.
I knew what I was looking at
but the map itself was quite lovely—
each island a star of luminous

blue that belonged to a much larger
constellation, and the entire world
shimmering with five constellations.

Then I remembered the water I
was drinking and understood that blue
moved through me, that I was radiant.

*Archipelago IV: Meditation Archipelago*

## Self-Defense

I bought a knife to have a knife. People
kept telling me
you must always have a knife.

They said: you can get one with a handle

carved with rubies
or the rarest pearls—your choice.

# Understory

All day I have been thinking of a tree
that yesterday
on a bank by the river

held one of its own branches in its arms.

*Like a mother*
I write—and then erase it.

## Meditation


Sixteen sugar packets. Yes, I counted.
I am alone
only one lifetime each day.

Yesterday was three earth-bruised tomatoes

the day before
twenty-seven cubes of ice.

*Pause*


You could be a Buddhist on a stalled train
surrounded by
stench and impatience, air close

as the last mouth you kissed, which was nowhere

near a subway
which was not, in fact, a mouth.

*Harvest*


Today I have not eaten. Tomorrow
I will visit
a friend's for dinner. Shall I

bring something? The meal, he says. And a box

or two of blue
ever-bearing hydrangeas.

*Leaf*


Something in you pushes past the others
crowded in this
shrub (like a boy taking leave

of a schoolyard of boys for some unknown

elsewhere) to be
studied—and possibly torn.

# Kinsale

And so you shall remain my might-have-been:
an if-only:
closed door in a hall of doors

mostly closed:    story hinted in the shroud

Penelope
wove each day to unravel . . .

## Miracle


Not the vagrant limping into traffic
dodging every
honk and swerve, but the woman

who watches, bites her bottom lip and waits

then draws him up
from the curb when he gets there.

## *Sadist Says*


Have you heard about the itinerant
masochist? He
was into vagabondage.

Once, wandering through the desert, he saw

an oasis
and hoped it was a mirage.

## On Second Thought


You cannot be the hermit of Hermit
Island. Hermit
Island is the hermit of

Hermit Island and, therefore, neither you

nor he could be
its hermit, should you live there.

# Flash Card



Recto: unicorn. Verso: flamingo.
Some forms exist
solely in a world of myth.

Others inhabit this world, but elsewhere.

Elsewhere are those
who have never felt paper.

# Document

Nothing in it needed to be in it
other than to
be in it to be in it.

Elsewhere     in the wish-I-was-where-you-are

rain weighed down stalks
of lupine. There were novels.

# Subtext

The myths tell us no one wants to cross paths
with a shaman
when that shaman is angry.

They do not say shamans get easily

angered because
no one crosses paths with them.

*Gaëtan*


No matter what the scribblers said, those who
met me wanted—
whether they knew it or not—

to kiss the purple island on my thigh.

This I allowed,
sighing free their unseen wounds.

*Fever*


The doctor says I am too sick to rise.
I fear I will
miss everything. A horse comes

to tell me I've missed nothing. He isn't

handsome but I
crave him: his tension, his neck . . .

*Lemon*


My niece, three, eats one whole. When her taste buds
develop she
will accept it only squeezed

or sliced, as if a practiced penitent

swaying, praying
for a partial glimpse of God.

# Self-Critique

God assesses the invention of sand.
He admits its
flaws are obvious: how it

will not hold its own against wind, how it

sticks to the skin
of His other great mistake . . .

# Three Pebbles

Side-by-side an old gypsy places them
on her table
before me: "The black one helps

to remember. The white one to forget.

This gray one is
useless. Carry it always."

## *Hostel*


I keep this little birdhouse on my desk
to remind me
I am—as so many are—

one paycheck shy of seeking charity.

Look: two windows:
both of them for flying in.

*Notes*

## I: And Then

The stanzas for "April 3, 2015," "Centerpiece," "Memo," "My First Memory," "Surfacing," "Swath," and "Word Problem" correspond with my zip code (14620). The first line in each stanza is one syllable; the second is four syllables; the third is six; and the fourth is two. Zero is represented by a break between stanzas.

The haiku grouped in "Haiku from the Other Hand" were written with my non-dominant hand.

"Memo" was inspired by an email from the Permanent Office of the International Holocaust Remembrance Alliance (IHRA). The concern outlined in the first lines of the poem was initially addressed to a division office of Microsoft Germany; it was then summarized in memo form for the Committee on Antisemitism and Holocaust Denial, and cascaded to select Holocaust and Human Rights Advocacy groups.

## II: Novaya Zemlya

"Novaya Zemlya": "rectangular suns" and "horizons shaped as hourglass" refer to the Novaya Zemlya Effect, a mirage first noted and explained by Gerrit de Veer on the ill-fated Willem Barents expedition of 1596–97.

## III: This Is Not an Exit

Several of the untitled, unrhymed, largely enneasyllabic sonnets in this section allude to events that were originally reported in *The New York Times*.

## IV: Meditation Archipelago

These syllabic poems are patterned on the postal code for Belushya Guba, Novaya Zemlya: 21 10 4 7.

"Gaëtan" refers to Gaëtan Dugas, or "Patient Zero," unfairly sensational-
ized as a sexual predator in Randy Shilts's *And the Band Played On.*

*Acknowledgments*


Thanks to these publications and their editors where the following poems appeared, sometimes in earlier versions. *The Bakery:* "Baltimore." *The Brooklyn Rail:* "Fever"; "Meditation"; "Miracle"; "Self-Defense"; "Subtext"; and "Three Pebbles." *Connotation Press (Poetry Congeries):* "April 3, 2015"; "Swath"; and "Word Problem." *EOAGH:* "By a Bend in the River." *Festival Writer (The Sestina Issue):* "Fortune Cookie" and "Raisin Bran and Sliced Tomatoes." *The Fourth River:* "Sablefish." *Great River Review:* "Short Story." *LIGHT/WATER:* "Pause" and "Sadist Says." *OCHO: A Journal of Queer Arts:* "Still Life" and "Surfacing." *Pencil Marks:* "Harvest" and "Leaf." *Prompt:* "After Watching Marco Berger's *Hawaii*" and "Haiku from the Other Hand." *The Prose Poem Project:* "September Song." *Provincetown Arts:* "Novaya Zemlya." *Sentence:* "Green Dolphin Street." *Star 82 Review:* "Hostel."

"Green Dolphin Street," "September Song," and "By a Bend in the River" were previously gathered in the chapbook *Fake Book,* Anything Anymore Anywhere Press, 2011.

"After Watching Marco Berger's *Hawaii*" was reprinted in *Image OutWrite 4.*

"Novaya Zemlya" and "Surfacing" received 2015 Pushcart Prize nominations.

The opening line of "Still Life" comes from the first line of Arthur Sze's poem "The Waking"; it is reprinted here with the author's permission.

Many thanks to the following who provided valuable feedback about these poems in various stages of their completion: Albert Abonado, Thomas Blake, Jeana Bonacci-Roth, Maria Brandt, Peter Conners, Steve Fellner, Michael Klein, Barbara Lovenheim, Peter Monacelli, Jorge Rodriguez-Miralles, Cathy Smith, James Tolan, Michael Waters, and of course Steve Huff, whose faith in me has meant more than words can say.

## *About the Author*

Tony Leuzzi's previous books include *Radiant Losses* (New Sins Press, 2010) and *The Burning Door* (Tiger Bark Press, 2014), and two chapbooks, *Fake Book* (Anything Anywhere Anymore Press, 2011) and *40,000 Crows* (Hank's Original Loose Gravel Press, 2012). In 2012, BOA Editions published *Passwords Primeval*, Leuzzi's interviews with 20 American poets. An Associate Professor of English at Monroe Community College in Rochester, NY, Leuzzi has received a Wesley T. Hansen Award for Excellence in Teaching and a State University of New York Chancellor's Award for Creativity and Scholarship. He has written reviews and criticism for *The Brooklyn Rail, Lambda Literary,* and *SCOUT Poetry,* among other places, and is a visual artist whose paintings incorporate collage and erasure.

# Colophon

The text of *Meditation Archipelago* was designed by Richard Foerster,
using Monotype Centaur and Bernhard Modern fonts.
The cover was designed by Phil Memmer.
Cover art is by Kathleen Farrell.
The publisher is Steven Huff
for Tiger Bark Press, Inc.

❖  ❖  ❖

The following people
contributed to the publication of this book:

Janet Ekis
John Fleming
Roger A Freitas
Melissa Hall
Barbara and John Lovenheim
Maureen Malone
Peter and Gloria Monacelli